WITHDRAWN FROM DEVON LIBRARIES

THE STEAMING SIXTIES

Stirring episodes from the last decade of Steam on BR

4. THE DAYS THAT WERE – THE WITHERED ARM IN CORNWALL
by Peter J. Coster

Copyright IRWELL PRESS Ltd.,
ISBN 978-1-906919-09-2
First published in 2009 by Irwell Press Ltd., 59A, High Street,
Clophill, Bedfordshire, MK45 4BE
Printed by KONWAY PRESS.

This book has a common thread in reminiscing about the fascinating railway that once ran through Devon into Cornwall, terminating at the Shangri-La of fish cuisine, Padstow. That common thread is the letter W. Think about it – West, Withered Arm, Wadebridge, Wenford, Well Tanks, Woolworths, er – Western, and yes, to many of us, Wonderful. My visits to the West Country, before I moved here, were opportunities to photograph a railway that was almost diametrically opposite to my daily experience on the electrified main lines, yet still a railway, with some common features. So these photographs tend to be bunched into certain dates, but still a reflection of many things that were going on at the time. The low speed and vagaries of colour film half a century ago have led to some wastage of precious shots, something that continues to irritate. The O2 0-4-4Ts had just gone, alas, displaced by Ivattisation with his excellent 2-6-2Ts. The marvellous little N 2-6-0s were still in evidence, and among the engines that I rode on, I had the particular privilege of riding on No.31837 on her last day in revenue earning service – so far as I know, that is. It was a very sad experience to ride on such a fine little engine that had years of good running in her, soon to be reduced to scrap by an accountant's pen. I can also claim to have ridden on both the very last up and down Atlantic Coast Expresses to and from Okehampton, on September 5th 1964, but the weather later was not good and few photographs were possible. By Padstow it was drizzling – perhaps even God was sad, too. The North Cornwall was a fine railway in difficult terrain, well engineered, and despite its distance from villages and towns, is still sadly missed. The Wadebridge-Padstow track is now the Camel Trail, and has more users than the railway ever did. It was one of the most beautiful stretches of railway on the system, and is ever more widely enjoyed today.

The book tends to concentrate on the Wenford Bridge branch and its freight service, for which I make no apology. I had a few shots of the Beatties, but on travelling on the line, the GWR panniers had just started work. The countryside was – and still is – remote and beautiful, and the railway was utterly basic and yet a common sense one. When the Beeching Report was officially launched upon BR staff, I remember my horror at the opening shot – a Beattie well tank chugging along through fields south of Helland Bridge. If the Good Doctor had stumbled on Wenford, the fat was well and truly in the fire. But it was a beautiful shot – I wonder whether it survives anywhere?

A colleague once asked me for my view on an accident report on the Wenford branch, relating how a new member of staff had broken an ankle turning rails at Tresarrett. When I asked what on earth men were doing working on the branch on a Sunday at double time, clearly I had trodden on a sensitive Western toe metaphorically, being unaware of the Western's Old Pals Act; I was told it was none of my business!

So come with me back to the days of the Withered Arm, to a railway that has inspired many a fine model layout such as the well known local one, Treneglos, that recaptures the days that were.

Peter J. Coster.
Pendoggett, Cornwall.

In August 17th 1962 the Wenford branch freight headed by No.1369 waits at Dunmere crossing while an ancient Leyland lorry heads for Wadebridge. There was just enough space between the trap points at Dunmere Junction and the level crossing for an engine and 29 wagons.

The 7.50 from Bodmin Road arrives at Wadebridge on August 17th 1962 behind none other than Crewe's 7,000th locomotive, No.41272, last seen on the Bedford branch a few years earlier. The 8.12 from Padstow is standing in Platform 2 behind one of the unlamented D6300 class diesel hydraulics, D6350.

Wadebridge's newly acquired No.1367 shunts the goods shed on August 17th 1962 while a group of shunters (an attachment?) discuss the affairs of the moment.

THE WENFORD BRANCH Part 1

On the Wenford goods on August 17th 1962 the fireman of No.1369 hands over the Wadebridge-Boscarne single line token at Boscarne Junction.

No.1369 with the Wenford goods on August 17th 1962, at Boscarne Junction. The goods ran forward towards Bodmin General on the ex-GWR line in order that the 9.50 Wadebridge-Bodmin North could pass on the ex-SR single line. The SR had converted some of the overhead DC electric stock into bogie brake vans which had met with great approval, and a new batch was built, I believe at Ashford. Wadebridge had 'come by' one of these, and as I had official permission to travel on the train, it was attached for my use!

The 9.50 Wadebridge-Bodmin North passes Boscarne Junction behind Ivatt 2-6-2T No.41272 on August 17th 1962. I wonder if Ramsbottom or Webb, in their wildest imaginations, ever thought that a Crewe locomotive would be working on a remote Cornish branch line?

A photograph too good to miss. Dunmere Crossing on August 17th 1962 with No.1369 waiting to charge across the A389. For decades this duty, No.607, later No.637, was the preserve of the three Beattie well tanks, but earlier in 1962 the three outside cylindered 0-6-0 pannier tanks were drafted in as replacements.

THE STEAMING SIXTIES No.4

No.1369 ambles warily across the A389 at the foot of Dunmere Hill. The guard has the presence of mind to stand in the lee of the train! A minor point, but the train was certainly not a stopping passenger and the lamp should have been on the lower iron. The reason was that the SR route code discs (see page 27) would not fit the GWR lamp irons (of course) and a GWR lamp was used instead. Not that it was a problem, since pedantic signalmen seemed not to exist in the West Country!

No.1369 taking water at Pengarhard Woods. A spring had been intercepted uphill from the line and channelled in troughing on to the structure shown. As can be seen, the business end of the troughing needed raising for the panniers, since the filler bag had to act as a siphon to get any water into the tanks. It is of course a timeless scene, or at least we thought so at the time, as fully three quarters of an hour was spent in taking water.

Still taking water. Possibly No.1369 was evaporating it quicker than the rate of supply. In the period of the great throwaway BR spent huge sums in eradicating the past, almost venomously and quite needlessly, and it is no surprise that the structure has long since disappeared without trace.

No.1369 heads up the Camel Valley in delightful country near Tresarrett.

The principal source of traffic on the line were the china clay dries at Stannon owned by the (then) English China Clay Lovering Pochin company. At the time fine clay was bagged and despatched in vans, and the rest went in sheeted wagons. The clay was piped down from Bodmin Moor and dried here. A stop block (similar to that in front of No.1367 at Wadebridge on page 3) was provided to prevent running away during shunting operations, and the train has stopped just beyond.

Like all dries, the site was smothered in blinding white china clay, which nearly caused cardiac arrest in the light meter. No.1369 draws the loaded vans and wagons out. The dries were old and no doubt expensive to run, with coal having to be brought from hundreds of miles away; even the discovery of fresh deposits of clay, on the moor, was not sufficient to prevent their closure.

Midday at Wenford Bridge on August 17th 1962. Time stands still. Even the gantry crane looked long disused. No.1369 slumbers in the sunshine while the crew, guard and shunter lunch in the guards van. It was a curious little terminal in the middle of beautiful but sparsely populated North Cornwall. The branch had a number of 'wharves' serving local farms, delivering sea sand and, in later days, agricultural and coal traffic. Wenford Bridge served the village of St.Breward and moorland farms. The bridge itself was a small, ancient arch bridge over the Camel, one of a few down the valley. The railway followed the Camel valley which turned towards Camelford north of here, on the North Cornwall line, so there was little point in going further.

No.1369 shunting at Wenford on August 17th 1962.

THE STEAMING SIXTIES No.4

The Wenford freight, now reassembled, is ready to depart for Wadebridge behind No.1369 on August 17th 1962. This picture marks the end of our first section, The Wenford Branch Part 1.

The 15.30 from Wadebridge pauses at Port Isaac Road on August 17th 1962 for a down service. The N class 2-6-0s were fondly referred to as 'Woolworths' in Cornwall, and one of these excellent little locos, No.31845, is the train engine. A short distance into the single line section lay Betty and Tom's Siding, serving Tregildrans Quarry, for which special traffic arrangements were specified. Betty was in fact a Mr Betty, co-owner of the quarry and not a spouse!

THE STEAMING SIXTIES No.4

The 15.13 Padstow-Exeter waits at Otterham on August 17th 1962 to cross the down ACE, hauled by No.34072 257 SQUADRON.

No.31845 rolls into Launceston on August 17th 1962 with the 15.30 from Wadebridge. A WR service from Plymouth via Tavistock has arrived behind 45XX No.4571. After the closure of the WR station, trains used the wartime link into the SR station.

The 16.40 from Torrington has arrived at Halwill Junction off the wonderfully named North Devon & Cornwall Junction Light Railway, and the signal is off for No.41290 to set back and run round her train in the loop some way outside the station. The ND&CJLR passed through remote but beautiful country and was extended by the SR from the original narrow gauge clay lines from Torrington to Peters Marland in 1925 under a Government funded scheme to reduce local unemployment, as witness the relatively new concrete platform. Meanwhile the 16.40 goods from Wadebridge approaches in the background behind No.31837. The return trip to Torrington at 18.30 connected with the 17.51 from Okehampton, which in turn connected with the 13.00 from Waterloo. The date is August 17th 1962; I was the only passenger on the 18.30.

BR 3MT 2-6-2T No.82022 eases into Halwill Junction with the 18.01 service from Bude. The signalman waits for the single line token from Holsworthy. 'Halwill Junction for Beaworthy' announced the station nameboards impressively in 1962, the paint of an unforgiving WR by then peeling off. The massive signalbox appeared to have space for control of the whole North Cornwall system. The date is August 17th 1962.

N 2-6-0 No.31837, with the 16.40 up freight from Wadebridge, drifts to a halt at Halwill Junction to await the 17.51 from Okehampton before resuming progress to Exeter on August 17th 1962. Halwill was another of those places with a surplus of lineside furniture behind the locomotive to frustrate the photographer.

A meeting of Woolworths at Halwill Junction on August 17th 1962. No.31875 with the 17.51 from Okehampton, connecting back to the 13.00 from Waterloo, runs into Halwill Junction while No.31837 has the 16.40 Exmouth Junction goods.

It is a warm sunny Devon evening and Ivatt 2-6-2T No.41290 pulls away from Hatherleigh with the 18.30 to Torrington on August 17th 1962.

Wadebridge shed with No.34078 222 SQUADRON in new company, panniers Nos.4694 and 1369 on September 16th 1962. Behind No.1369 was the remaining Beattie well tank, No.30587. Apparently the 57XX panniers were not well received at Wadebridge. The 1366 class were fine on the Wenford branch, but at anything faster than a gentle jog on the running line they gave a good impression of a rocking horse.

Callington station, in the finest railway tradition, was not at Callington but Kelly Bray. On September 16th 1962 Ivatt 2-6-2Ts Nos.41214 and 41216 are at Callington's small sub-shed with the station and its unique overall roof in the distance.

The Wenford goods arrives at Wadebridge in September 1958 behind No.30585; station pilot No.30586 waits nearby.

The odd one of the Beattie trio, No.30586, in its usual role as station pilot at Wadebridge, September 1958. The 2-6-0 for the 16.40 goods is going on to the turntable in the distance. No.30586 was formerly No.3329 of the Southern Railway, and while her sisters were Beyer Peacock engines with curved splashers, she retained the square splashers of the Nine Elms-built engines. As we have seen, the engine on the Wenford goods (the famous Duty 607, later 637) took water from a diverted spring feeding the water tower in Penhargard Woods. The well tank of the Beatties held only 550 gallons and in dry weather it took an eternity, as mentioned already. On No.30586 the filler cap on the bunker had been raised as an experiment to prevent coal falling in, but it meant that she could not take water reliably at Penhargard on the Wenford branch. As a result she was only used on the Wenford turn in emergency. Beyond the 2-6-0 is the LNWR 12 wheel coach, improbably labelled 'Work Study' which was at Wadebridge in the last years.

BR 4MT 2-6-4T No.80042, off the Bude service, stands in Halwill yard on September 9th 1963. The building behind is the abattoir, with conflats standing behind. The Bude stock stands in the down bay.

THE STEAMING SIXTIES No.4

The Atlantic Coast Express heads west towards Halwill behind No.34083 605 SQUADRON on September 16th 1963. LYDFORD's later prominence in this book aside, one of the oddities in latter years was that most of the Bulleid light Pacifics in the West Country were Battle of Britains, with the denizens of Kent and Sussex left to puzzle the whereabouts of such curious names on the West Countries. The result was that the passengers were confronted with locomotives bearing the name of a squadron whose name meant something to RAF types and nothing to anyone else.

N 2-6-0 No.31856 couples on to the empty stock of the 13.05 Padstow-Exeter Central on September 20th 1963.

N 2-6-0 No.31839 runs round the stock of the 10.12 from Okehampton at Padstow on September 20th 1963.

No. 41275 with the 14.52 from Padstow at Wadebridge on September 20th 1963.

Ivatt 2-6-2T No.41275 with the 9.50 from Wadebridge passes Boscarne Junction on September 20th 1963. Boscarne ground frame, which controlled access to/egress from the exchange siding, is on the right.

No.1367 was often used on freight duty. This included shunting Wadebridge wharf on the bank of the Camel, which lay beyond the level crossing. Here No.1367 is at Wadebridge on September 20th 1963; its tyres look down to scrap size... A new Type 2 diesel hydraulic is in platform 3.

The 16.40 freight for Exmouth Junction has been made up and is ready to leave Wadebridge behind 'Woolworth' 2-6-0 No.31844 on September 20th 1963.

No.31844 leaves Wadebridge for the east, with a tender well filled with dust, on the 16.40 freight for Exmouth Junction on September 20th 1963.

On September 20th 1963 Ivatt 2-6-2T No.41275 was working the service between Padstow and Bodmin North, Exmouth Junction Duty 598. Here she is running round her two car set at Padstow to form the 14.52 to Bodmin North. Little of the railway remains today in the vast car park that this site has become, although the Southern's old hotel, the Metropole, still stares out across the Camel.

THE WENFORD BRANCH Part 2

The Wenford goods sets off with No.1369 from Stannon dries on May 5th 1964.

The Wenford branch originally had a number of 'wharves' along its length for unloading sea sand, which was then used by farmers to break up the heavier clay soil inland. One such was at Tresarrett, where No.1369 has paused on May 5th 1964. Tresarrett was still in use, as was Helland Bridge and Dunmere, but the others had been disused for a long while.

Cornwall in springtime, with No.1369 approaching through Dunmere Wood on May 5th 1964.

Wadebridge's bogie brake was out for another airing on May 5th 1964; here it is being propelled across Dunmere Crossing under the supervision of Shunter Harry Knight.

A group from the Stephenson Locomotive Society had arranged to visit the Wenford branch on May 5th 1964, and we were delighted to find that Driver Norman Wills had ensured that No.1369 was gleaming for the occasion. Part of the down train had been pinned down and left behind for loading timber pit props. It had been recoupled, giving the appearance at Dunmere of a GWR type 'motor train', but for freight. The ganger makes for home and tea.

THE STEAMING SIXTIES No.4

No.1369 at Wadebridge on May 5th 1964. This picture marks the end of The Wenford Branch Part 2.

Ivatt 2MT 2-6-2T No.41275 coasts into Grogley Halt with the 14.52 from Padstow on May 8th 1964. The platform is built of standard Exmouth Junction reinforced concrete units. I suspect that it dates back to the closure of the Ruthern Bridge branch in the 1930s; it had joined the Bodmin-Wadebridge line at this point and, as a result, the track was realigned and a new platform constructed.

Bodmin North, or as we now call it, Sainsbury's, was a delightful little terminus that has no doubt sired many a model railway layout. On September 20th 1963 Ivatt 2-6-2T No.41275 was working between Padstow and Bodmin North. Here she is running round to form the 16.23 to Padstow.

No.41275 running round at Bodmin North, to head the 16.23 to Padstow, on May 8th 1964.

Late in the steam era a new freight service was introduced wherein traffic from the ex-SR lines, usually china clay, was worked to Fowey via Bodmin General. No.31842, with a miniscule load, waits in the exchange sidings at Boscarne Junction on May 8th 1964 for the 15.30 Bodmin Road-Wadebridge, before departing for Bodmin General. On the ex-SR line the 14.52 Padstow-Bodmin North was not far off, and the Wenford goods was held for it at Dunmere Junction, on the branch.

No.41275 on the 14.52 Padstow-Bodmin North passes No.31842, waiting on May 8th 1964 for the Wenford goods in the exchange siding at Boscarne Junction.

258 miles from Waterloo, No.34106 LYDFORD draws to a halt at Padstow with the Atlantic Coast Express on May 8th 1964.

The view from Padstow coal dock as the 18.00 Padstow-Exeter crosses the Iron Bridge hauled by N 2-6-0 No.31837.

The 18.12 from Wadebridge was usually a single coach, and the Bulleid light Pacific off the down Atlantic Coast Express was used, first running light from Padstow to Wadebridge to pick up her train. It was the example much loved by critics of the number and use – or misuse – of the Bulleid Pacifics, but in fact it was a sensible use of resources. No.34106 LYDFORD was the loco, and the date May 8th 1964.

The Camel estuary is a truly beautiful sight on a sunny day, and the loss of the Wadebridge-Padstow line remains one of the bitterest blows, aesthetically, of the Beeching years. Of course the Camel Trail, its replacement, is hugely popular nowadays. The most distinctive feature remains the 'Iron Bridge', spanning the entrance to Little Petherick Creek, which attracted a heavy speed restriction. On May 8th 1964 the view from the monument on Dennis Hill was superb, but when No.34106 LYDFORD, earlier off the ACE, departed tender first for Wadebridge with her single coach, alas, I had failed to anticipate that the train would be completely enclosed in the ironwork of the lattice girders.

The up Atlantic Coast Express behind No.34106 LYDFORD pauses at St.Kew Highway on May 9th 1964. Although four Bulleid coaches might not be thought a taxing load for the Pacific, on the 1 in 75 grades the engine was worked hard and the coal consumption was surprisingly high.

The up Atlantic Coast Express waits at Otterham with No.34106 LYDFORD.

THE STEAMING SIXTIES No.4

The up Atlantic Coast Express behind No.34106 LYDFORD runs into Halwill on May 9th 1964. No.41249 with the 8.52 from Torrington stands in the bay used by services on the elegantly named North Devon & Cornwall Junction Light Railway.

Ivatt 2-6-2T No.41322 draws away from attaching the two coaches from Bude to the Padstow portion of the ACE on May 9th 1964. The Torrington one coach train stands in the North Devon bay behind sister engine No.41249.

BR 2-6-4T No.80064 on the 10.00 from Okehampton arrives at Halwill Junction, crossing the up Atlantic Coast Express behind No.34106 LYDFORD on May 9th 1964.

The up Atlantic Coast Express behind No.34106 LYDFORD waits at Halwill Junction for a down train in the single line section on May 9th 1964.

THE STEAMING SIXTIES No.4

No train for hours on end, but when someone wants to use the level crossing one comes along! So might the tractor driver be thinking but I doubt he is in a hurry. No.34106 LYDFORD sets off from Halwill Junction with the Atlantic Coast Express on May 9th 1964 in suitably rural surroundings.

In happier days, on September 20th 1963, No.31853 ambles into Okehampton with a tiny up freight. Although Okehampton's little shed was only a sub of Exmouth Junction, there was plenty of activity, with re-manning and the provision of motive power for North Cornwall trains.

A view from the footbridge at Wadebridge on September 5th 1964 with No.1368 on the 16.20 school train to Padstow. This was often worked by the station pilot. Wadebridge level crossing is in the distance, and the old Bodmin and Wadebridge offices and workshops are to the left of the line. The area is now a Co-Op supermarket and car park, and part of the station building survives as the Betjeman Centre.

THE STEAMING SIXTIES No.4

On March 27th 1965, when steam had been all but eliminated from the West Country, a train of Meldon ballast coasts down from Dartmoor behind No.34007 WADEBRIDGE. The ballast is carried in the ex-SR Walrus 40 ton bogie hopper wagons, with two 25 ton Dogfish as the second and third vehicles.